Inspirational Quotes FOR TEENS

"Inspirational Quotes FOR TEENS "

Daily Wisdom to Boost Motivation, Positivity, and Self-Confidence

Christopher Taylor, MA, LMFT

ROCKRIDGE
PRESS

To all the teens who have inspired me over the past 20 years, and to my brother, who taught me to focus on what is possible.

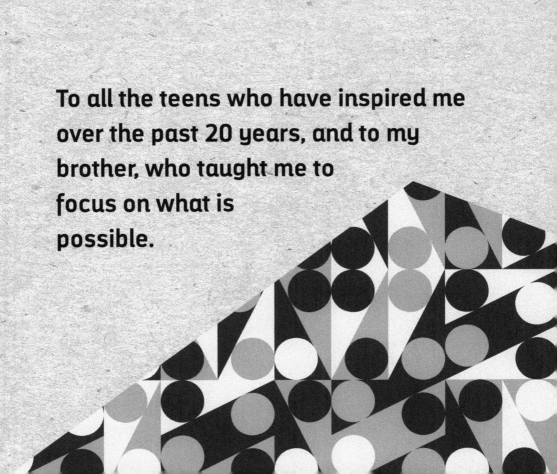

Introduction

Imagine the feeling of pride and self-confidence that comes from achieving one of your biggest goals, like being accepted to your first choice of colleges, receiving an award for your art, or simply being able to identify all your positive qualities. Feeling good about yourself doesn't happen by accident, and you can make it happen. When you focus on what inspires you, only good things can follow.

If you are wondering if this book is for you, let me assure you it is. Over the past 20 years I have provided counseling and therapy services to teens just like you. But it was before that professional journey that I learned the power of inspiration. After dealing with feelings of depression, anxiety, and low self-worth, I realized I had to change my mindset to change my life. That realization led me to understand the transformational power of inspiration.

When we are inspired, we unlock our full potential. We use our natural abilities and gifts to create, to help, and to change the world. You have that power within yourself. Having a strong sense of self-confidence will enhance every other area of your life. Your relationships improve, people trust you and seek out your ideas, and you give the gift of inspiration to others. It's a vibe that becomes contagious!

So how do you find inspiration? It doesn't need to be through traveling to Neptune or curing cancer, though I believe you could do those things. Inspiration can also be found in wanting to improve your artistic abilities by painting that flower you saw on the walk home. Maybe you find inspiration in seeing an older person struggling to carry their groceries, so you volunteer to help them on weekly shopping trips. It doesn't matter how big or small, only that you fully believe in what you are doing.

This book is intended to help you explore life and find inspiration in many ways. You will find quotes from people you know and admire that will serve as encouragement. There will also be off-the-page activities that will help you uncover passions and interests. There is no right or wrong way to use this book. You can read it in order or open to a random page. It is really that simple.

I challenge you to use this book to find one thing that inspires you today and take action toward that idea. Now that is inspirational!

Once you believe in who you are and who you were born to be, it can be very powerful.

—DWAYNE JOHNSON

"I don't think dreams magically appear, that's why they're called dreams. But if you do want to make that dream a reality, then you have to push yourself. It takes a lot of hard work.

–GABBY DOUGLAS

> **I can accept failure, everyone fails at something. But I can't accept not trying.**
>
> —MICHAEL JORDAN

3

> I think that process of performing at my best is very addictive. Once you see what you're truly capable of, it is eye-opening.
>
> —ALYSSA AZAR

What I have learned in this life is you can never be ashamed of where you come from.

—TYLER PERRY

I cannot allow myself to live in fear.
You don't really live, if you live in fear.

—TONI HARRIS

> **Keep exploring. Keep dreaming. Keep asking why. Don't settle for what you already know. Never stop believing in the power of your ideas, your imagination, your hard work to change the world.**
>
> —BARACK OBAMA

"I don't know where bravery comes from. Maybe you're just born with it. For me, bravery happened because I don't like the feeling of being afraid; I much preferred the feeling of being strong, so when I thought something might be scary, I would go after it and tackle it head-on before it got the better of me.

—JESSELYN SILVA

> Don't let the noise of others' opinions drown out your own inner voice.
>
> —STEVE JOBS

"I created this from nothing, and I want to see how far I can take it.

—ASHLEY QUALLS

Inspiration Finds You

Let's take some time to do something fun that will help you find inspiration. First, wherever you are now, close your eyes and take three deep, slow breaths. Now open your eyes and look around. Be sure to go slow and take your time. What jumps out at you? Whatever you feel drawn to, make note of the connection. What does it say to you? How does it make you feel? Was it the shape, or the color? Notice that the things you are drawn to touch the place of inspiration inside you. By honoring these connections, we discover inspiration in all places.

> "Come out and work hard every single day, because you don't know what level of play you can get to by just starting at that moment right there . . . just go all out.

—TIANA DOCKERY"

> **The visionary starts with a clean sheet of paper, and re-imagines the world.**
>
> —MALCOLM GLADWELL

"You have to remember that the hard days are what make you stronger. The bad days make you realize what a good day is. If you never had any bad days, you would never have that sense of accomplishment.

—ALY RAISMAN

14

> **Every day is different, and every day brings something more exciting.**
>
> —MICHAEL PHELPS

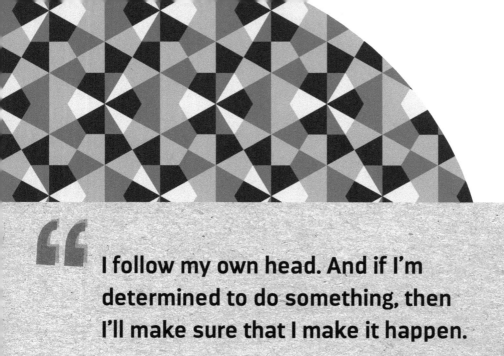

"I follow my own head. And if I'm determined to do something, then I'll make sure that I make it happen.

—LAURA DEKKER

> **Don't be part of the spectacle, be truthful about what you care about and speak from the heart.**
>
> —DAVID HOGG

17

> **The main thing is to care. Care very hard, even if it is only a game you are playing.**
>
> —BILLIE JEAN KING

"

I really do believe
that as young people
we can make an
enormous difference.
All we have to do is
take action.

—NICHOLAS LOWINGER

"

"Go for it—you don't have that much to lose. Even if it goes downhill, there's always a lesson.

—CHARLOTTE FORTIN "

"Just let everyone know that you are amazing. Do not let anyone hate on you. You are a superstar.

—DESMOND NAPOLES

21

The Mindful Walk

Today I encourage you to go for a walk in your neighborhood. As you walk, take note of every sound you hear, every sensation you feel on your skin, and all the things you see. Try to stop and really see things in a new way. For example, pick up a leaf from the ground and look at its color. Take note of the texture in your fingers, the smell as you bring it to your nose. When you take the time to stop and observe, your mind slows down and finds joy and wonder in simplicity.

"

The more I'm able to empower myself,
the more I can do things that sustain
the world as a whole.

—KELVIN DOE

"

"Choose bravery over perfection. Just get started and accept that you will make mistakes and might end up looking silly. But you will be moving towards whatever matters most to you and learning. If you get too focused on trying to do something perfectly, you probably will never start.

—JADE HAMEISTER

"Stay focused, determined, and if you have issues explaining yourself at times, just think about how you really feel, how much you really want to inspire others.

—JAYLEN ARNOLD"

> My advice is just to begin. When you see a need, act. Dream big, but start small, taking little steps.

—MARY GRACE HENRY

26

> I want to go out there and do some different things that people are like, 'Wow. That's crazy. Why didn't I think of that?'

—JUSTIN BIEBER

" I think my positive attitude has really helped me run my business. There were bumps in the road along the way, but I knew I had to stay strong and keep moving forward. "

—MADISON GREENSPAN

> We all have dreams. But in order to make dreams come into reality, it takes an awful lot of determination, dedication, self-discipline, and effort.

—JESSE OWENS

"Innovation is what we need, right? And I think that comes from all ages. I think we all have a different perspective and that allows us to create amazing products.

—ALISSA CHAVEZ

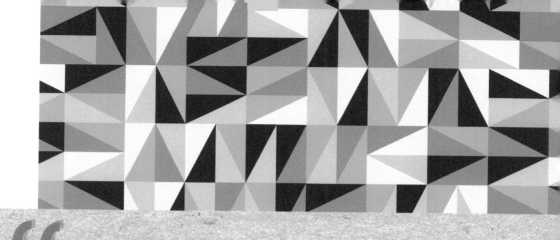

> **If you want to live a happy life, tie it to a goal, not to people or objects.**
>
> —ALBERT EINSTEIN

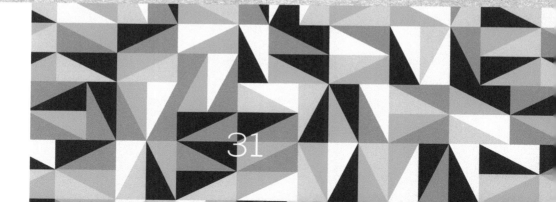

31

If you have a dream, you should just go for it. Just go running toward it.

–KHERIS ROGERS

Explore Your Strengths

Have you ever felt like there is nothing good about you?
Let's challenge that belief. Take out a sheet of paper
and write down all the things you can come up with
in these three categories: what you're good at, what
you like about yourself, and what you're interested in,
even if you haven't tried it. Are you adventurous? Do
you enjoy music? Are you athletic or artistic? After you
think you've written down everything you can think of,
I want you to write down at least 10 more things. Then
try to add one more thing each day.

"

I've learnt that no one is too small to make a difference.

–GRETA THUNBERG

34

> **If you actually do something you love, it's a lot easier and takes on a lot more purpose.**
>
> —MARK ZUCKERBERG

35

So many times we look outwardly for acceptance or validation, and I think it takes a certain amount of strength and boldness to say, 'You know what, I am going to believe in myself and I believe I am enough to activate myself.' It's a decision and a mindset you really have to commit to.

—HAILE THOMAS

"

We will all face
challenges but
you cannot let any
challenge stop you
from achieving
your purpose.

—WILLIAM KAMKWAMBA

"

"I believe age is just a number. If you have an idea, no matter how old you are, you have the power to change the world.

—SAMAIRA MEHTA"

> **Determination, persistence, realism, wanting success more than your next breath— that's the key to success. I mean it's so simple!**
>
> —LOGIC

39

> **" I feel like I'm truly and genuinely proud and unafraid. I'm not scared of who I am. "**
>
> —DRAKE

40

"Changing the world, to me, means removing stereotypes, and most importantly not forgetting about the hidden force of women. In the 21st century, we can't just stand by when women are left out and intimidated.

—SABINA LONDON

41

"I don't think it's your age that determines the potential you have. It is the unlimited imagination that you have that gives you the unlimited potential to create.

—ELIF BILGIN"

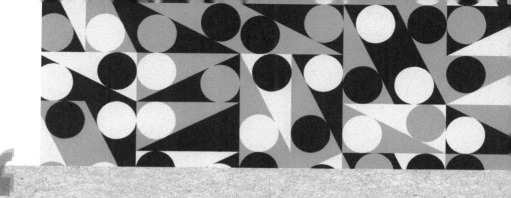

> **People should pursue what they're passionate about. That will make them happier than pretty much anything else.**
>
> —ELON MUSK

43

Find Your True Power

Our subconscious mind is programmed with the messages we give ourselves about who we are. If the messages are negative, then we might feel like we don't deserve good things or that we shouldn't try anything new because we believe we'll fail. But, if we tell ourselves positive thoughts about ourselves, then we remove limitations from what we can achieve. So how do we program our minds? Simply follow this exercise: Write down the words "I am" and follow them up with a positive adjective to describe yourself. Then go to a mirror, look yourself in the eye, and say the statement with confidence and appreciation. The more times you do this, the more confidence you'll feel.

You have to do what's best for you and what's going to make you happy at the end of the day, because no one can live with the consequences or anything that comes with your decision besides you.

—LEBRON JAMES

"Nothing is impossible and it's important to try to achieve your goals. But you have to be prepared to work hard and learn to take criticism and not let that criticism be the reason for not making things happen.

—BELLA TIPPING

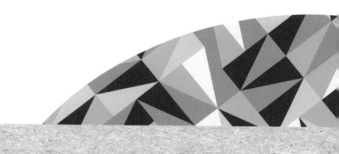

> **When we have a good balance between thinking and feeling . . . our actions and lives are always the richer for it.**
>
> —YO-YO MA

47

> "You're going to go through so many things, but you have to never give up. You can't give up because you're a child. And you can't be afraid to fail. That's one thing that I've learned.

—ASIA NEWSON

"

I don't look at obstacles as obstacles. I look at them as things that were put there for a reason. You can approach these things negatively or positively. I think those that approach it with a negative mindset only get a negative outcome.

—KEVIN HART

"

49

> **The most creative people are the ones who step out of their comfort zone and take advantage of the world around them.**
>
> —KYEMAH MCENTYRE

Some of my greatest
pleasures have come
from finding ways to
overcome obstacles.

—JOHN WOODEN

"I want girls to believe in themselves, to feel like we are powerful, we are strong, that we have the capability to do anything. It's okay to be you and you don't have to change for anybody.

—TAYLOR RICHARDSON

"For me, I'm focused on what I want to do. I know what I need to do to be a champion, so I'm working on it.

—USAIN BOLT

53

"Whenever I see something that desperately needs to be changed, I create an app for it. My goal isn't to change the world. I just hope to change the people who live in it.

—AMANDA SOUTHWORTH

54

Giving Thanks

Often, we focus on what isn't going well or what we don't have. When we do that, we allow ourselves to get bogged down in negative thinking. This clouds our minds and prevents us from being present and joyful. Instead, let's learn to focus on what we are thankful for. I challenge you, for the next 30 nights, to write down three things you are thankful for. These can be anything you want, as long as you're genuinely thankful for them. Also, try not to write the same thing twice. Now go get your mind focused on appreciation and being grateful.

"Be intentionally self-aware, flexible, and brave. Self-awareness means understanding who you are as an individual and what unique gifts you bring to the world. Being flexible will help you deal with disappointments and setbacks in business and in life. Being brave is essential to discovering your purpose.

—TANIA SPEAKS

> **If you want to soar like an eagle in life, you can't be flocking with the turkeys.**
>
> —WARREN BUFFETT

" "

Create your own path,
hone your talent, be
ready to show your talent,
and don't doubt yourself.

—ICE CUBE

" "

58

> **It's just about people on the forefront saying, 'I'm willing to stand up and make a difference.'**
>
> —AURORA JAMES

"

It's never too early to start. There is no better time than now to be a female founder. Be curious, ask questions, build things, and ignore the notion of boundaries. You'll be surprised to see how many people will want to join you for the ride and help you along the way.

—CAROLINE PUGH

"

> When you have been
> given the wave, you
> have to ride it.
>
> —SHAWN MENDES

"Even when it's not pretty or perfect. Even when it's more real than you want it to be. Your story is what you have, what you will always have. It is something to own.

—MICHELLE OBAMA"

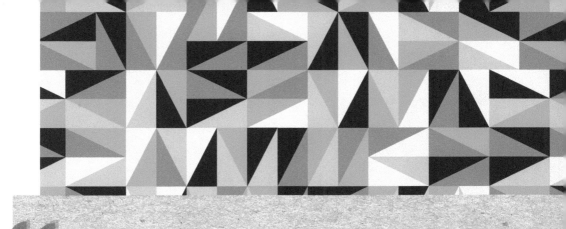

> **It's like I'm waking up into the new discovery of myself.**
>
> —KHALID

63

"Kids are not 'the future,' we are here now. We are not going to change the world 'someday,' we are already doing it.

—ALLIE WEBER"

"

I've always considered myself to be just average talent and what I have is a ridiculous insane obsessiveness for practice and preparation.

—WILL SMITH

"

Overcome Your Fears

Fear is the thief of experiences. We often give in to our fears at the expense of opportunities for enjoyment. It is no easy feat to overcome these fears, but today let's take a first step in that direction. First, take out a piece of paper and pen. In the middle of the paper, write down what you are most afraid of. Write it big and in all caps—after all, that fear may really be that big in your mind! Now fold the paper in half, then in half again. Then rip it into tiny pieces while saying out loud, "[Your fear], you no longer have power in my life! I am done giving in to you, and now I am saying goodbye." Throw those torn pieces away and commit yourself to challenging that fear anytime it comes up by reciting that same sentence. You will be surprised at how powerful this exercise can be.

"I admire people who really talk in-depth or advocate for things they believe in but I want to be able to show people that it's okay to just be yourself.

—CAVETOWN

67

> **There's so much beauty in every note and there's so much to be discovered.**
>
> —CICELY PARNAS

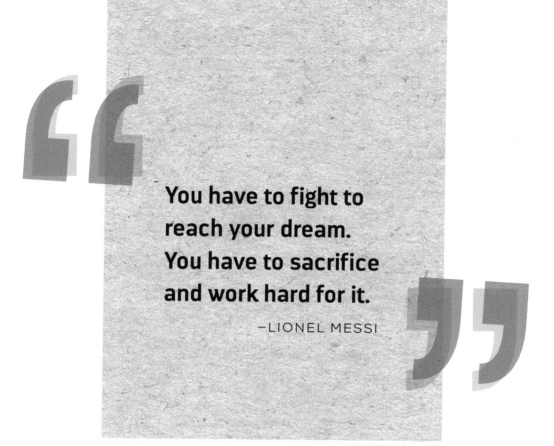

You have to fight to
reach your dream.
You have to sacrifice
and work hard for it.

—LIONEL MESSI

"

When you start thinking positive,
getting that negative out can change
your whole reality.

—NLE CHOPPA

"

> "By bringing diverse people together we can really solve some of the world's most complex problems because each person, based on their different backgrounds, can bring their different ideas to the table and you can solve problems in different ways.

—MIRACLE OLATUNJI

> "I can't imagine a life that doesn't involve creativity, or at least inspiring other people."
>
> —BILLIE EILISH

"My advice to teens is to try and do something that scares you every day because it's the only way you can test how far you can really go. Whether it's going out and auditioning for the play or trying out for the basketball team, you have to explore your boundaries and see where you really want to go, and the only way you can do that is to break out of your shell.

—ZAC EFRON

73

"In order to make anything a reality, you have to dream about it first. In many ways, our audacity to imagine helps push the boundaries of possibility.

—ADORA SVITAK
"

> You always, always, always have to start with a passion because if you don't have a passion, a love or drive behind what you're doing, then eventually it's going to go downhill, and you won't want to do it anymore. It's really important to do what you love because you'll go farther.
>
> —MAYA PENN

"I think defeat helps you more than success. I just do whatever I can to be better and learn from the mistakes.

—PATRICK MAHOMES"

Helping Hands

We spend a lot of time working for ourselves. Whether it's the things we want or the activities we enjoy, we can easily get self-consumed. But remember, it's better to give than to receive, so today find an opportunity to help someone else. It could be helping someone carry their groceries, mowing your neighbor's lawn, or putting the dishes away without being asked. Simply find someone around you who needs a helping hand and provide the help. After you do, pay attention to your feelings. Do you feel uplifted and inspired? Those feelings are there for you anytime you lend a helping hand.

"

I want to make my own
path and leave behind a
good legacy for myself
and honestly, I just want
to be innovative . . .
That's what I want to be
remembered by. I want
to inspire.

—A$AP ROCKY

"

> " So, we are speaking up for those who don't have anyone listening to them, for those who can't talk about it just yet, and for those who will never speak again. We are grieving, we are furious, and we are using our words fiercely and desperately because that's the only thing standing between us and this happening again. "

—X GONZÁLEZ

"You don't have to be a rocket scientist to change the world, you don't have to have Albert Einstein's hair, it doesn't matter where you come from, no matter your race, your sexuality, your socioeconomic background. The only thing that matters is how willing you are to dream. Don't be afraid to make mistakes.

—TRISHA PRABHU "

"
Let no feeling of
discouragement prey
upon you, and in the end
you are sure to succeed.

—ABRAHAM LINCOLN
"

81

> **Invention, it must be humbly admitted, does not consist in creating out of void, but out of chaos.**
>
> —MARY SHELLEY

> **No matter what people tell you, words and ideas can change the world.**
>
> —ROBIN WILLIAMS

"In any form of creativity, self-expression, or art, you're giving away a little part of yourself. You're confessing and owning up to insecurities, desires, ideas embarrassingly ambitious, ideas embarrassingly normal. You're owning up to being a real person.

—TAVI GEVINSON

**Run when you can,
walk if you have to,
crawl if you must;
just never give up.**

—DEAN KARNAZES

85

> **You are a role model, even if you aren't fully aware of that fact.**
>
> —CHARITIE ROPATI

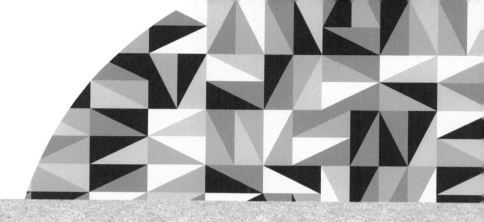

> **Perhaps you will forget tomorrow the kind words you say today, but the recipient may cherish them over a lifetime.**
>
> —DALE CARNEGIE

If You See It

When you create a vision for your life, your subconscious mind perceives it as having already happened. Not only that, but your brain changes the area that is active. Instead of using the part responsible for immediate gratification, it uses the part responsible for creating and executing long-term plans. Let's get to envisioning! Sit or lie down in a comfortable position and visualize your future self. What will you be doing? Where will you be living? Get as detailed as you can. Imagine your friends, lifestyle, clothes, surroundings. The more detailed you can be, the more impactful the vision will be. There's no need to limit yourself or play it safe. This is about truly believing that all things are possible and that you can achieve even your wildest dreams.

"

Have a heart that never hardens, and a temper that never tires, and a touch that never hurts.

–CHARLES DICKENS

"

> I learned that courage was not the absence of fear, but the triumph over it. The brave man is not he who does not feel afraid, but he who conquers that fear.

—NELSON MANDELA

90

"

Being a young woman in STEM, I often feel the need to set a role to those even younger than me, to show them that even in a male-dominated field we have the capability to make a huge impact. As women in STEM, we are creating our own path, proving along the way that our gender won't prevent us from reaching success.

—MEGHNA BEHARI

"

"I want to challenge you all to find what it is that you're passionate about, that makes you excited and motivates you. It can be anything, whether it is volunteering, sports, reading, anything! I challenge you to go out and do it. Use your energy for good. Who knows, you might even change the world!

—CASSANDRA LIN"

> Find out who you are, be comfortable with it, embrace it, and let that be the most consistent thing that you can . . . rely on.

—STEPHEN CURRY

"

**Indulge your imagination
in every possible flight.**

—JANE AUSTEN

"

> To all trans people who deal with harassment, self-loathing, abuse, and the threat of violence every day: I see you, I love you, and I will do everything I can to change this world for the better.
>
> —ELLIOT PAGE

"

My parents are not involved in science. But they always told me I had the ability. They said if you do the research and you have the passion, you can do anything.

—KIARA NIRGHIN

"

" I'm everything and nothing at all. I'm black, I'm white, I'm male, female. To me, seeing all the facets of yourself is the next level of our evolution—understanding who we really are.

—RUPAUL "

"

I try to give people a
different way of looking
at their surroundings.
That's art to me.

—MAYA LIN

"

What Fills You Up?

There are things in this world that fill you up with hope, love, and inspiration. These are the things that bring true enjoyment to your life. Hanging out with friends, cooking your favorite meal, reading a book—the possibilities are infinite. Today, do one of these small things, but instead of doing it casually, have the intentional thought, "I am doing this because I love myself and I deserve it." Simply taking actions in the name of self-love sends a clear message to yourself that you are worth it. And you truly are!

> **My call to action to all Brown girls (and beyond) out there: Be an active and engaged member of every community to which you belong. Be grateful for what you have. Empower yourself and empower those around you. Every human being has the potential to be a force for positive social change.**
>
> —RITU RAMAN

I know that you cannot live on hope alone, but without it, life is not worth living. And you . . . And you . . . And you . . . Gotta give 'em hope.

—HARVEY MILK

> **Touching people's lives in a positive way is as close as I can get to an idea of religion.**
>
> —KEITH HARING

"Success is not achieved by winning all the time. Real success comes when we rise after we fall. Some mountains are higher than others. Some roads steeper than the next. There are hardships and setbacks, but you cannot let them stop you. Even on the steepest road you must not turn back.

—MUHAMMAD ALI

> "Just don't give up trying to do what you really want to do. Where there is love and inspiration, I don't think you can go wrong.

—ELLA FITZGERALD

**Anything I do,
I want to do it well.**

−J. COLE

105

"I encourage teens to go after what they love and not worry about their age, because the rewards of talking about things that are important to them while expanding their own knowledge are incredible!

—MAYA VAN WAGENEN

> **We are taught to understand, correctly, that courage is not the absence of fear, but the capacity for action despite our fears.**
>
> —JOHN MCCAIN

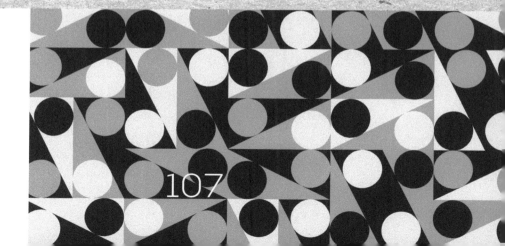

107

"What I kind of want to spread as my message to all kinds of youth that I get to reach out to is, you can do cool stuff, you've just got to put in time and be dedicated."

—ANN MAKOSINSKI

> I feel like people are expecting me to fail, therefore, I expect myself to win.
>
> —LEWIS HAMILTON

Let Loose

Time to have fun! Go through your playlists and pick out the most energetic and upbeat song you can find. Play that song and turn it up loud! (If you're using speakers, be aware of anyone around you, and if you're using headphones, keep the volume below 75 percent to protect your ears.) Feel the music and give in to the emotion it creates. Sing out loud if you know the words or dance freely no matter where you are. Ignore any insecurities or internal voices telling you not to. Give in to this simple act of pure joy. When you fully engage in this moment of fun, you will find freedom and peace.

"Sometimes you gotta go with your first instinct. You gotta go with your gut. That's kind of how I live my life, you gotta go with your gut.

–MICHAEL B. JORDAN

111

" For me, dance is about the aesthetics and the hard work that goes into creating something so beautiful. Motivation and dedication to the craft is what pushes me to do my best, to always strive to do better, and the outcome is always worth it. "

—YUAN YUAN TAN

"Sometimes some of the toughest things you deal with end up being the best things because you realize the people that you can rely on, that love you, and support you through it.

—TOM BRADY

113

"

Because I learned long ago that winning doesn't always mean you get the prize. Sometimes you get progress, and that counts.

—STACEY ABRAMS

"

" All right—we're gonna do what we can. And I'll give what I can. Connecting with other human beings is the thing that gives me hope in the end.

—CHASE STRANGIO

"

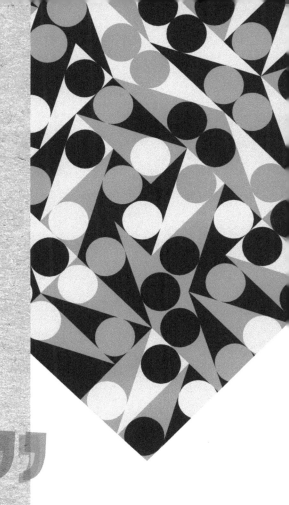

" I knew then and I know now that, when it comes to justice, there is no easy way to get it. You can't sugarcoat it. You have to take a stand and say, 'This is not right.' And I did.

—CLAUDETTE COLVIN "

"If there's something that I can do, or something that I can share, that is going to save a life, or make people's lives better and encourage others, and empower others to come forward to share their own story as part of their own healing process, [I'm] kind of willing to do anything.

—PRINCE HARRY

117

"Security is mostly a superstition . . . Avoiding danger is no safer in the long run than outright exposure. The fearful are caught as often as the bold. Faith alone defends. Life is either a daring adventure or nothing."

—HELEN KELLER

118

"

The secret is to make your mind work for you, not against you. This means constantly being positive. Constantly setting up challenges you can meet either today, next week, or next month. 'I can't . . .' should be permanently stricken from your vocabulary, especially the vocabulary of your thoughts. You must see yourself always growing and improving.

—ARNOLD SCHWARZENEGGER

119

"Focus on what it is that you want, set a realistic goal. Start setting goals that you feel you can accomplish . . . Every time you accomplish a goal you develop the strength and wisdom to accomplish the next one.

—CHUCK NORRIS

Ground Yourself

When we feel stress, it often consumes our thoughts. Our mind takes over and keeps us focused on things beyond our control. It also takes us away from being fully present in that moment of our life. To counter that, follow this simple practice of self-awareness. Starting at the top of your head, mentally scan your body for where you are holding on to stress. Is your jaw clenched? Are your neck or shoulders tense? Is your stomach uneasy? Maybe your legs or feet are tight? As you find the areas where you're holding stress, take a deep breath through your nose for five seconds and let the oxygen go right to the area of discomfort. Then exhale slowly through your mouth for five seconds, and imagine you are exhaling that tension as you breathe out. Repeat these deep breaths three to five times.

"

A lot of young people think they have no power, they can't control what's going on. We can choose who we want to elect, and we can be the ones running for office. I want to see more action and less talking.

—NAOMI WADLER

"

> "You are ready and able to do beautiful things in this world . . . you will only ever have two choices: love or fear. Choose love, and don't ever let fear turn you against your playful heart.

—JIM CARREY

"I raise up my voice—not so I can shout but so that those without a voice can be heard . . . we cannot succeed when half of us are held back.

—MALALA YOUSAFZAI

"

All your dreams can come true if you have the courage to pursue them.

—WALT DISNEY

125

> "There are so many trans kids who are struggling with who they are. I want them to know that one day, they will find the light. No matter what, we have to be who we are. Once you love and accept yourself, then others will slowly do so as well.

—JAZZ JENNINGS

> **It's a lie to think you're not good enough. It's a lie to think you're not worth anything.**
>
> —NICK VUJICIC

"

We need to remember that our ancestors' prayers are still protecting this land, and that we are our ancestors' hope. One day I will be an ancestor, and I want my descendants to know I used my voice so they can have a future.

—AUTUMN PELTIER

"

> **If you don't enjoy it, don't do it.
> You must love what you do.**
>
> —RICHARD BRANSON

"There really isn't anything special about me, and I honestly believe that anyone who has the passion and drive to alter the status quo really can elicit change. It's hard work, but anyone can do it if they feel strongly enough.

—AMIKA GEORGE

130

> "There is hope. There are stories, people, and resources out there to help you. You're not alone."
>
> —PARAM JAGGI

References

Abrams, Stacey. "Voting Feels Inadequate Right Now." *The New York Times*, June 5, 2020. NYTimes.com/2020/06/04/opinion/stacey-abrams-voting-floyd-protests.html.

Agence France-Presse (AFP). "Girl, 14, OK to Sail Solo Around the World." Emirates247.com. July 28, 2010. Emirates247.com/lifestyle/travel/girl-14-ok-to-sail-solo-around-the-world-2010-07-28-1.272064.

Ahmed, Insanul. "The Winning Formula: How Logic Found the Key to Success." Complex.com. November 13, 2015. Complex.com/music/2015/11/how-logic-found-his-winning-rap-formula.

Ali, Muhammad. *Muhammad Ali Unfiltered: Rare, Iconic, and Officially Authorized Photos of the Greatest*. New York: Simon & Schuster, 2016, p. 88.

Arnold, Jaylen. "How to End Bullying for Good: Interview with Jaylen Arnold." World of Children. October 2, 2014. WorldofChildren.org/interview-jaylen-arnold.

Austen, Jane. *Pride and Prejudice*. Edited by Vivien Jones. London: Penguin Classics, 2003.

Bieber, Justin. "Interview: Justin Bieber Talks About His Top 5 Rappers, Selena Gomez, and Growing Up in the Game." Interview by Joe la Puma. Complex.com. March 30, 2012. Complex.com/music/2012/03/interview-justin-bieber-talks-about-his-top-5-rappers-selena-gomez-and-growing-up-in-the-game.

Biggs, Mary, ed. *Women's Words: The Columbia Book of Quotations by Women*. New York: Columbia University Press, 1996, p. 66. Google.com/books/edition/Women_s_Words/mgMKMWzuVRkC?hl=en&gbpv=0.

Bolt, Usain. The Internet Movie Database. IMDb. IMDb.com/name /nm3118048/bio.

Bonioli, Sara. "Obama To Young Scientists: 'Keep Asking Why.'" HuffingtonPost .com. March 23, 2015. HuffPost.com/entry/obama-white-house-science -fair_n_6925836. Commencement Address at Stanford University, delivered June 12, 2005, Palo Alto, CA.

Branson, Richard. "Richard Branson's Five Rules for Business." CNBC. August 2, 2012. CNBC.com/id/48469449.

Brown Girl Magazine. "Brown Girl of the Month Dr. Ritu Raman Builds Our Biohybrid Future." March 12, 2018. BrownGirlMagazine.com/2018/03 /brown-girl-of-the-month-dr-ritu-raman-builds-our-biohybrid-future.

Cap, Damon. "Madison Greenspan of Maddie Rae's Slime Glue—Exclusive Interview." BSC Kids. February 6, 2018.

Carnegie, Dale. *The Quick and Easy Way to Effective Speaking*. New York: Diamond Pocket Books Pvt Ltd., 2017, p. 153.

Carrey, Jim. "Commencement Address at Maharishi International University (formerly Maharishi University of Management) in Fairfield, Iowa." May 24, 2014. MIU.edu/graduation-2014.

Choppa, NLE. "NLE Choppa Talks Battling Depression, Music Collabs, and His True Feelings about the Black Lives Matter Movement." Interview by Shirley Ju. Revolt.tv. October 15, 2020. Revolt.tv/2020/10/15/21518025 /nle-choppa-music-interview.

Chung, Becky. "This 13-Year-Old Entrepreneur Is Out to Change the World: A Q&A with Maya Penn." Ideas.TED.com. January 27, 2014. Ideas.TED.com /maya-penn-entrepreneur.

Clifford, Catherine. "What You Can Learn about Success from This Girl Boss Who Started Her Own Clothing Business at Age 10." CNBC. August 7, 2018. CNBC.com/2018/08/06/flexin-in-my-complexion-co-fou nder-kheris-rogers-advice-on-success.html.

Cole, J. "J. Cole: An Upstart Rapper Speaks for Himself." Interview by Robert Siegel and Guy Raz. *All Things Considered.* NPR. November 1, 2011. NPR.org/transcripts/141910346.

Cube, Ice. "The 'Barbershop: The Next Cut' Interview." Interview by Kam Williams. TheSkanner.com. April 12, 2016. TheSkanner.com/entertainment /people/23693-the-barbershop-the-next-cut-interview.

Curry, Stephen. "Future Hall of Famer Stephen Curry, Whom So Many Doubted, Is Headed Home for All-Star Game." Interview by David Dennis Jr. TheUndefeated.com. February 14, 2019. TheUndefeated.com/features /future-hall-of-famer-stephen-curry-whom-so-many-doubted-is -headed-home-for-all-star.

Cutler, Jaqueline. "Bergenfield Boxer Jesselyn Silva Knocks Out a Memoir, *My Corner of the Ring*." June 7, 2019. NJ.com/entertainment/2019/06 /bergenfield-boxer-jesselyn-silva-knocks-out-a-memoir-my-corner -of-the-ring.html.

D'Souza, Delano. "The More I'm Able to Empower Myself, the More I Can Do Things that Sustain the World as a Whole." France24.com. September 30, 2019. France24.com/en/20190930-perspective-kelvin-doe-emerging -engineer-sierra-leone-africa.

Deitch, Jeffrey, Suzanne Geiss, and Julia Gruen. *Keith Haring*. New York: Rizzoli, 2008, p. 505.

Dickens, Charles. *Our Mutual Friend*. New York: Cosimo, 2009, p. 455.

Drake. "HipHop Canada Interview." HipHopCanada.com. July 12, 2006. HipHopCanada.com/2006/07/drake-interview.

Efron, Zac. "EXCLUSIVE: Zac Efron and Vanessa Anne Hudgens Sing Their Praises for *High School Musical*." Movieweb Interview. Movieweb.com. May 22, 2006. Movieweb.com/exclusive-zac-efron-and-vanessa-anne -hudgens-sing-their-praises-for-high-school-musical.

French, A. P., ed. *Einstein: A Centenary Volume*. London: The International Commission of Physics Education, 1979.

Gevinson, Tavi. "Introduction." Poetry Foundation. Accessed March 10, 2020. PoetryFoundation.org/poetrymagazine/articles/70230/introduction -56d249ff643b8.

Gladwell, Malcolm. "The Tweaker." *The New Yorker*. November 6, 2011. NewYorker.com/magazine/2011/11/14/the-tweaker.

Goalcast. "Top 12 Most Inspiring Malala Yousafzai Quotes." March 7, 2017. Goalcast.com/2017/03/07/top-12-most-inspiring -malala-yousafzai-quotes.

Haines, Tim. "David Hogg: You Need to Realize That Washington D.C. Is a 'Spectacle,' Don't Be a Part of It." RealClearPolitics.com. March 23, 2018. RealClearPolitics.com/video/2018/03/23/david_hogg_we_need_to _realize_that_washington_dc_is_a_spectacle.html.

Hall, Macey. "Aly Raisman's Tips for Going After What You Want." *Seventeen*. May 23, 2013. Seventeen.com/health/advice/g561/aly-raisman -interview/?slide=2.

Hamilton, Lewis. "Interview: Lewis Hamilton." Interviewed by Serena Williams. InterviewMagazine.com. July 19, 2017. InterviewMagazine.com/culture /lewis-hamilton.

Hart, Kevin. "A Heart-to-Heart with Kevin Hart." Interview by Dave Itzkoff. *The Chicago Tribune*. digitaledition.ChicagoTribune.com/tribune/article _popover.aspx?guid=8a0b1a6f-e805-4977-a9ed-6e4866d672c6.

Harrington, Samantha. "How High School Founder Miracle Olatunji Is Democratizing Opportunity." *Forbes*. January 16, 2018. Forbes.com /sites/samanthaharrington/2018/01/16/how-high-school-founder -miracle-olatunji-is-democratizing-opportunity/#273973ce2154.

Henry, Mary Grace. "Interview with Mary Grace Henry, founder of Reverse The Course." World of Children. September 23, 2014. WorldofChildren .org/interview-mary-grace-henry-founder-reverse-course.

Hislop, Madeline. "Meet Alyssa Azar: The Youngest Australian to Climb Mt. Everest, Twice." Women's Agenda. May 22, 2019. WomensAgenda .com.au/latest/meet-alyssa-azar-the-youngest-australian-to-climb -mt-everest-twice.

Hoose, Phillip. *Claudette Colvin: Twice Toward Justice*. New York: Farrar Straus Giroux, 2009.

Hunter, Leah. "The 13-Year-Old Entrepreneur Changing the Face of Business in Detroit." *Forbes*. January 10, 2017. Forbes.com/sites/leahhunter /2017/01/10/the-13-year-old-entrepreneur-changing-the-face -of-business-in-detroit/?sh=600f910d1f1d.

Ignotofsky, Rachel. *Women in Science: 50 Fearless Pioneers Who Changed the World*. Berkeley: Ten Speed Press, 2016.

Jaggi, Param. "Why Not???!!–Param Jaggi." Interview by The Common Girl. June 20, 2015. TheCommonGirl95.WordPress.com/2015/06/20/why -not-param-jaggi.

James, Aurora. "Aurora James on How Big Retail Can Support the Black Community." Interview by Edward Enninful. *TIME*. September 15, 2021. Video, 2:36. TIME.com/collection/100-most-influential-people-2021 /6095806/aurora-james. Accessed December 5, 2021.

James, Lebron. "The Decision" with Jim Gray. ESPN. July 9, 2010. ESPN.com /blog/truehoop/post/_/id/17853/lebron-james-decision-the-transcript.

Jennings, Jazz. "What Jazz Jennings Wants All Trans Kids to Know." *TIME*. March 31, 2016. Time.com/4275809/jazz-jennings-transgender-rights.

Jobs, Steve. Commencement address. Transcript of speech delivered at Stanford University, June 12, 2005. News.Stanford.edu/2005/06/14 /jobs-061505.

Johnson, Dwayne. "Mythical Proportions: An Exclusive Interview With Dwayne 'The Rock' Johnson." Interview by Matt Tuthill. MuscleandFitness .com. MuscleandFitness.com/athletes-celebrities/interviews/mythical -proportions-exclusive-interview-dwayne-rock-johnson.

Johnson, Jazzi. "Toni Harris Talks to Blavity on Making History as the First Woman to Receive a 4-Year Football Scholarship." Blavity. March 1, 2019. Blavity.com/video/toni-harris-talks-to-blavity-on-making-history-as -the-first-woman-to-receive-a-4-year-football-scholarship.

Jordan, Michael, and Mark Vancil. *I Can't Accept Not Trying: Michael Jordan on the Pursuit of Excellence*. New York: Harper, 1994, p. 129.

Jordan, Michael B. "Michael B. Jordan Talks Gold Temptation, 'Fantastic Four' Reboot & More!" TheSource.com. August 13, 2014. TheSource.com/2014 /08/13/michael-b-jordan-talks-gold-temptation-fantastic-four -reboot-more.

Kamkwamba, William. "A Kern County Family Magazine Interview: Q&A with William Kamkwaba." Interview by Callie Collins. *Kern County*

Family Magazine. November 1, 2019. KernCountyFamily.com/Articles
-Special-Feature-i-2019-11-01-127296.113117-A-Kern-County-Family
-Magazine-Interview-QandA-with-William-Kamkwamba.html. Accessed
December 1, 2021.

Karamali, Kamil. "UBC Student Ann Makosinski Wins $50K for Phone-Charging."
CBC News, December 22, 2015. CBC.ca/news/canada/british-columbia
/ubc-ann-makosinski-phone-charging-mug-1.3377735. Accessed
December 5, 2021.

Karnazes, Dean. *Ultramarathon Man: Confessions of an All-Night Runner*.
New York: Penguin, 2006, p. 197.

Keller, Helen Adams. *The Open Door*. Garden City, NY: Doubleday, 1957.

Khalid. "Khalid Talks High School Prom, Going Platinum, and Getting a New
Puppy." Interview by Carino Chocano. *Vogue*. July 20, 2018. Vogue
.com/article/khalid-interview-vogue-july-2018.

Kip, Alex. "Robin Williams: Genie in the Lamp." HuffingtonPost.com. August 14,
2014. Huffpost.com/entry/robin-williams-genie-in-t_b_5676511.

Kramer, Jillian. "The Secret to My Success: How Haile Thomas Launched a
Heathy Eating Nonprofit." *Food & Wine*. February 23, 2018. FoodandWine
.com/news/halie-thomas.

Krohn, Katherine, E. *Ella Fitzgerald: First Lady of Song*. Minneapolis, MN:
Lerner Publications, 2001, p.7. Google.com/books/edition/Ella_Fitzgerald
/pLBEVVf69K0C?hl=en&gbpv=0.

Lin, Cassandra. "My Name Is Cassandra, This Is My Story . . ." My Name My
Story. Accessed March 10, 2020. MyNameMyStory.org/cassandra-lin.html.

Lincoln, Abraham. *The Collected Works of Abraham Lincoln*. Rockville, MD:
Wildside Press, 1953, p. 87.

Ma, Yo-Yo. "Exclusive Interview with Yo-Yo Ma on the Spirituality of Music." Interview by Laurence Vittes. HuffingtonPost.com. September 30, 2012. HuffPost.com/entry/yo-yo-ma_b_1920286.

Mandela, Nelson. *Notes to the Future: Words of Wisdom*. New York: Simon & Schuster, 2012, p. 18.

McCain, John, and Marshal Stalter. *Why Courage Matters: The Way to a Braver Life*. New York: Ballantine Books, 2008.

McEntyre, Kyemah. "This Girl's Homemade Prom Dress Is the Most Incredible Thing You'll See Today." *Marie Claire*. June 10, 2015. MarieClaire.co.uk/news /kyemah-mcentyre-s-homemade-prom-dress-beats-the-bullies-72728.

McRae, Ellie. "Interview with Bella Tipping." Kebloom. July 22, 2018. Kebloom .com/inspiration/2018/8/23/interview-with-bella-tipping.

Mendes, Shawn. "Shawn Mendes: 'The Fear Strangled Me. I Really Fell Down'." Interview by Simon Hattenstone. *The Guardian*. December 9, 2020. TheGuardian.com/music/2020/dec/09/shawn-mendes-the-fear -strangled-me-i-really-fell-down.

Milk, Harvey. *The Harvey Milk Interviews: In His Own Words*. Edited by Vince Emery. Vince Emery Productions, 2012.

Musk, Elon. "Elon Musk AskMen Interview." Interview by Jim Clash. AskMen.com. AskMen.com/entertainment/right-stuff/elon-musk-interview-4.html.

Nicols, Alexis. "11-Year-Old Coder Samaira Mehta on Reverse Ageism, Gender Gap." *Parentology*. October 29, 2019. Parentology.com/11-year-old-coder -samaira-mehta-on-reverse-ageism-gender-gap.

Norris, Chuck. "An Interview with Chuck Norris." Interview by Geoff Thompson. Physical Arts.com. PhysicalArts.com/en/culture/interviews/an-interview -with-chuck-norris.

Obama, Michelle. *Becoming*. New York: Crown, 2018, p. xi.

Owens, Jesse. Archive.NYTimes.com/www.nytimes.com/learning/general
/onthisday/bday/0912.html.

Page, Elliot. "Elliot Page Is Ready for This Moment." Interview by Katy
Steinmentz. *Time*. March 16, 2021. Time.com/5947032/elliot-page-2.

Patterson, Denny. "Desmond Is Amazing: LGBTQ Youth's Number-One
Advocate." OutFrontMagazine.com. June 3, 2021. OutFrontMagazine
.com/desmond-is-amazing-lgbtq-youths-number-one-advocate.

Pellot, Emerald. "This 22-Year-Old Is on a Mission to Provide Homeless Youth
with Footwear." Yahoo.com. January 21, 2021. Yahoo.com/lifestyle/22
-old-mission-homeless-youth-220454818.html.

Peltier, Autumn. "Why Have So Many Communities Gone Without Water
for So Long, Autumn Peltier Asks." TheTyee.ca. September 30, 2019.
TheTyee.ca/Opinion/2019/09/30/Autumn-Peltier-Asks-Why-So-Many
-Communities-Have-No-Water.

Perry, Charlie. "Junio Tiana Dockery (Navajo) Returns to (22) Kansas
Jayhawk Volleyball Looking to Improve on Last Season's Sweet 16 Run."
NDNSports.com. August 22, 2014. NDNSports.com/junior-tiana-dockery
-navajo-returns-to-22-kansas-jayhawk-volleyball-looking-to-improve
-on-last-seasons-sweet-16-run.

Perry, Tyler. *Don't Make a Black Woman Take off her Earrings*. New York:
Riverhead Books, 2007.

Phelps, Michael. "How the Dramatic Ups and Downs of Fame Have Made
Michael Phelps a Better Father." Interview by Quinn Keany. PopSugar.com.
June 24, 2017. PopSugar.com/celebrity/Michael-Phelps-Save
-Water-Interview-2017-43655962.

Popova, Maria. "Brainpickings." Accessed March 26, 2020. LiteraryJukebox
.brainpickings.org/post/44644231776.

Pugh, Caroline. "This College Student Tracks Your Body as You Workout and
Lose Weight." *Forbes*. December 9, 2013. Forbes.com/sites/deniserestauri
/2013/12/09/this-college-student-tracks-your-body-as-you-workout
-and-lose-weight/#64892ea85679.

Quotabelle. "Cicely Parnas" Accessed March 10, 2020. Quotabelle.com
/author/cicely-parnas.

Rae, Kareem. *I Want to Become a Professional Soccer Player: The Ultimate
Guide for a Soccer Player to Go Pro*. Amazon Publishing, 2019, p. 64.
Google.com/books/edition/I_WANT_TO_BECOME_A_PROFESSIONAL
_SOCCER_P/nOAsEAAAQBAJ?hl=en&gbpv=1.

ROCKY, A$AP. "A$AP ROCKY on His Debut Album 'LONG.LIVE.A$AP' and
Upcoming NZ show." Interview by Shahlin Graves. *Coup de Main Magazine*.
June 12, 2013. CoupDeMainMagazine.com/interviews/interview-asap
-rocky-his-debut-album-longliveasap-upcoming-nz-show.

Rodriguez, Victoria. "11 Empowering Quotes from Emma González."
Seventeen. March 15, 2018. Seventeen.com/life/school/a19433627
/emma-gonzalez-quotes.

Ropati, Charitie. "Q & A with 2019 Champion for Change, Charitie Ropati."
Center for Native American Youth, February 4, 2019. CNAY.org/__
trashed-8. Accessed December 5, 2021.

RuPaul. "Oprah Talks to RuPaul About Life, Liberty and the Pursuit of
Fabulous." Interview by Oprah Winfrey. Oprah.com/inspiration/oprah
-talks-to-rupaul#ixzz74yvy8Z49.

Salter, Chuck. "Girl Power." *Fast Company*. September 1, 2007. FastCompany
.com/60278/girl-power.

Schofield, Emma. Jacada. "Women in Travel Series Interviews: Jade Hameister." JacadaTravel.com/the-explorer/women-travel-series -interview-jade-hameister.

Schwarzenegger, Arnold, and Douglas Kent Hall. *Arnold: The Education of a Bodybuilder*. New York: Simon & Schuster, 1993, p. 148.

Scipioni, Jade. "Chiefs Quarterback Patrick Mahomes: 'Defeat Helps You More Than Success.'" CNBC.com. April 15, 2021. CNBC.com/2021/04/15 /chiefs-patrick-mahomes-i-think-defeat-helps-you-more-than -success.html.

Shelley, Mary. *Frankenstein or the Modern Prometheus*. London, 1818. Reprint G. Routledge & Sons, London, 1888. Google.com/books/edition/Frankenstein _Or_The_Modern_Prometheus/2QwWAAAAYAAJ?hl=en&gbpv=0.

Shontell, Alyson. "Mark Zuckerberg's 8th Grade Speech." BusinessInsider.com. June 9, 2011. BusinessInsider.com/mark-zuckerbergs-8th-grade-speech -2011-6.

Shutler, Ali. "Cavetown: Bedroom-Pop Hero Building Worldwide Community." NME.com. July 10, 2020. NME.com/blogs/nme-radar/cavetown-bedroom -pop-hero-building-worldwide-community-2705382.

Smith, Will. "Interview: Will Smith." Interview by Todd Gilchrist. IGN.com. December 18, 2006. IGN.com/articles/2006/12/18/interview-will -smith?page=1.

Society for Science and the Public. "These 8 Young Women Prove STEM Isn't Just for Boys." November 6, 2017. SocietyForScience.org/blog/these-8 -young-women-prove-stem-isnt-just-for-boys.

Strangio, Chase. "Trump's War on Trans Rights: A Q&A with Chase Strangio." Interview by Naomi Gordon-Loebl. *The Nation*. November 9, 2018. TheNation.com/article/archive/chase-strangio-interview-trans-rights.

Sutton, Megan. "Meet the Inspiring Young Women Campaigning to End Period Poverty, Champion Girls' Education and Protect Animal Rights." *Good Housekeeping*. July 3, 2019. GoodHousekeeping.com/uk/news/a26618418/teenage-activists-campaigners-international-womens-day.

Svitak, Adora. "What Adults Can Learn from Kids." TED. TED.com/talks/adora_svitak/transcript?language=en#t-148580.

Teen Vogue. "21 Under 21 2017: See Photos and the Full List." December 15, 2017. TeenVogue.com/story/21-under-21-2017.

Thimmesh, Catherine. *Girls Think of Everything: Stories of Ingenious Inventions by Women*. Boston: Houghton Mifflin, 2018, p. 39. Google.com/books/edition/Girls_Think_of_Everything/a6lvDwAAQBAJ?hl=en&gbpv=0.

Thunberg, Greta. *No One Is Too Small to Make a Difference*. New York: Penguin Books, 2018.

TIME. "TIME's 25 Most Influential Teens of 2018." December 10, 2018. Time.com/5463721/most-influential-teens-2018.

Time Out Hong Kong. "Tan Yuan Yuan on Balanchine's Serenade, Striving for Perfection and the Hong Kong Ballet Scene." June 6, 2016. TimeOut.com/hong-kong/dance/tan-yuan-yuan.

Tom Brady Press Conference at Gillette Stadium. Courant.com. January 22, 2015. Courant.com/sports/football/hc-tom-brady-patriots-transcript-0123-20150122-story.html.

Vujicic, Nick. "Overcoming Hopelessness." MotivationMentalist.com. May 24, 2014. MotivationMentalist.com/2014/05/24/overcoming-hopelessness -by-nick-vujicic.

We Tech. "Wind Up for Wound Up." August 16, 2012. WeTech-Alliance.com /2012/08/16/wind-up-for-wound-up.

Weber, Allie. Twitter. June 21, 2017. Twitter.com/RobotMakerGirl/status /877638915162857473.

Weinberg, Lindsay. "2017 Honoree Sabina London." 22 Under 22. Accessed March 10, 2020. 22under22.HerCampus.com/2017/2017/10/4/sabina -london.

Whiting, Kate. "Top Quotes from the Young Change-makers at Davos." World Economic Forum. January 24, 2020. WeForum.org/agenda/2020/01 /top-quotes-from-davos-young-change-makers.

Williams, Kam. "Gabby Douglas: Raising the Bar." *The New Orleans Tribune*. Accessed March 11, 2020. TheNewOrleansTribune.com/gabby-douglas -raising-the-bar.

Williams, Pat. *How to Be Like Walt: Capturing the Disney Magic Every Day of Your Life*. Deerfield Beach, FL: Health Communications, 2004.

Winfrey, Oprah, and Prince Harry. "Oprah and Prince Harry on Mental Health, Therapy and Their New TV Series." Interview by Mary Louise Kelly, Elena Burnett, Courtney Dorning. NPR.org. May 21, 2021. NPR.org/2021 /05/21/999229547/-this-is-a-service-to-the-world-oprah-and-prince -harry-on-new-mental-health-series.

Wooden, John, and Jay Carty. *Coach Wooden's Pyramid of Success Playbook*. Ada, MI: Revell, 2005, p. 50.

Wright, Travis. "7 Powerful Leadership Lessons from Warren Buffett." BusinessInsider.com. November 11, 2014. BusinessInsider.com/leadership -lessons-from-warren-buffett-2014-11.

Yako Books. "Popular Week: Interview with Maya Van Wagenen." May 31, 2015. YakoBooks.Blogspot.com/2015/05/MayaVanWagenenInterview .html.

YouTube. "Be You: Taylor." June 29, 2018. YouTube.com/watch?v=5sTJlCzzSQA.

YouTube. "Going Bananas: Redefining Plastics: Elif Bilgin at TEDxVienna." December 9, 2013. YouTube.com/watch?v=4LGTBzmrysM.

YouTube. "ReThink Before the Damage Is Done: Trisha Prabhu: TEDxYouth@ Hewitt." February 24, 2017. YouTube.com/watch?v=StqRJhHNUGA.

Acknowledgments

First off, a huge thank-you to my wife for allowing me late nights full of ramblings and good coffee and the space to put in the care needed to produce a book I am proud of. Thank you to my daughters, who had to sacrifice some daddy time so I could sit and work without interruptions: I can't wait to get back to made-up games and movie nights. And special thanks to the team at Callisto Media and Rockridge Press for the opportunity to create something that I hope inspires a lot of young people.

About the Author

 CHRISTOPHER TAYLOR, MA, LMFT, is a licensed marriage and family therapist who has specialized in working with teens for the past 20 years. At one year old he experienced the abandonment of his father, at age five his mother left the family due to her severe mental illness, and at 19 his only sibling, an older brother, passed away. It was in these losses that Taylor found his purpose to help heal and inspire young people to meet their own challenges head-on. He is an author and accomplished speaker, but he has no greater joy than being a husband to his amazing wife and father to his two incredible daughters.

CPSIA information can be obtained
at www.ICGtesting.com
Printed in the USA
BVHW021342200122
626692BV00003B/6